The Very Important Assignment

Dedicated to ALL of my loved ones.

Especially to my wife Nicole and to my daughters Andrea and Cecelia.

Thank you for supporting me and being my inspiration.

The Very Important Assignment

Written by
Anthony L. Surrette

Illustrated by
Ani Barmashi

Mrs. Hughes loved being a first-grade teacher at Johnson Elementary School.

Although her students were still little, she believed it was important to teach them life lessons.

"We will be having our career day next week. Who is excited to hear that?" asked Mrs. Hughes.

"What is a career?" asked a soft voice from the third row.

The voice belonged to a little brown haired girl, who had raised her hand tentatively. Her name is Natalie.

"A career is something you do as work to earn money when you grow up," responded Mrs. Hughes.

"In order to prepare for the day, you will be given a very important assignment.

It will be about what you want to be when you grow up." Mrs. Hughes continued.

"Please draw yourself in the career of your choice. Make sure to think about it and have fun!"

The bell rang, signaling the end of the day and the children trooped out of the class.

Natalie walked to the sidewalk and hopped into her dad's waiting car.

"Hello, sunshine!" exclaimed Natalie's father, Fred. "How did your day go?"

"It was alright," Natalie responded and continued staring out the window of the car.

"It is the weekend, aren't you excited? You are unusually quiet," said a concerned Fred.

"Mrs. Hughes gave us an assignment to draw a picture of what we want to be when we grow up, and I have no idea of what to do," Natalie responded sadly.

Fred smiled and said, "I know someone who might be able to help, but first let's get ice cream."

Natalie loves ice cream, especially the flavors from the little shop near Madison Park.

"Dad, can we go to Creamy Cone?"

"Yes, we can! I hear they have a new flavor mix that you will absolutely love," said Fred.

Natalie's face brightened up. "I hope it has chocolate in it," she said happily.

Fred parked the car in front of the ice cream shop, and they both went in.

Moments later, Natalie came out with a rainbow colored ice cream cone in one hand.

Her other hand was holding her father's hand and she could not have been happier.

They both had smiles on their faces as they headed back to their car.

They resumed the trip and for the better part of the drive, Natalie focused on her ice cream.

Fred looked at her from time to time and smiled.

The Hilly Meadows was their next stop, where they both loved spending time together.

Natalie loves feeding the ducks in the stream and walking around the fields with her father.

"We're here, sunshine," Fred said.

Natalie looked around and shouted, "Yay! The Hilly Meadows."

Fred parked the car and helped Natalie out of her seat.

The pair left the car and headed to their favorite spot under an old maple tree.

They sat in front of the duck pond and watched the ducks play in the water.

"They are so beautiful. Can I feed them?" Natalie pleaded.

Fred handed her the pack of bread crumbs from his pocket,

which she eagerly started throwing to the ducks.

"Do you know why this place is always clean, despite all the people that come here?" Fred asked.

"Yes, dad. The men in the blue uniforms keep the place clean," Natalie answered.

"Mrs. Hughes taught us to always use the bin, because dirt is bad for our environment.

I try to never throw trash on the ground," Natalie said proudly.

"That's a good girl," said Fred. "We should all do our part by not throwing trash on the ground."

"Do you know what a career is?" questioned Fred.

"A career is something you do when you're a grown up," Natalie answered quickly.

"Mrs. Hughes told us in class. She knows everything," said Natalie.

"I just can't think of any ideas for what I may want to do for a career." Natalie sadly stated.

"Well I can try to help!" said Fred.

"A career is a job or profession that you do because you have an interest in it," said Fred.

"It is something that you are excited about doing.

A lot of people will do the same job for many years," Fred continued.

"That will be so boring. I don't want to do the same thing for the rest of my life!" Natalie exclaimed.

Fred smiled. "It won't be boring if it's something you love doing and are passionate about."

"You mean like feeding ducks? I love doing that. Can that be my career?" asked Natalie.

"You can be a veterinarian. They take care of all kinds of animals," said Fred.

"Will I get to touch the ducks' feathers and make them shiny?" asked Natalie.

"As a veterinarian, you help give animals medicine and fix their injuries," responded Fred.

"Dad, look what I found. A four-leaf clover!" Natalie exclaimed picking the leaf from the ground.

"WOW! Did you know four-leaf clovers bring good luck to their finders?" asked Fred.

"But they are so hard to find, so how will people get lucky?" Natalie asked.

"I want to have a big factory that will make four-leaf clovers.

That way everybody can get them, and they can all have good luck," Natalie said.

"Another career you could choose is an accountant.

You can help people keep track of their money and good fortune," smiled Fred.

"What about the four-leaf clovers?" Natalie asked.

"As an accountant, people will trust you with their financial information.

You will bring them good luck by helping them organize their money." Fred said with a smile.

As they walked across a bridge, Fred said, "Did you know this bridge was designed by an architect?"

"Oh! What's an Archee…?"

"Architect. They design buildings like our house, your school, and even this bridge.

They can design almost anything," said Fred.

Natalie was thoughtful for a while. Then she asked, "Can they design mountains?"

"If I was an architect, I would design the most stunning and striking mountains.
They would be all different shapes and sizes," Natalie continued.

"That is a wonderful thought, but I don't think architects can do that," Fred responded.

"Why not?" asked Natalie.

"Mountains are usually formed naturally from many things.
But I am sure you could design many beautiful structures as an architect," said Fred.

Natalie and Fred loved staring at the clouds and the way they changed their shapes.

"Look, that one looks like a race car! That one looks like a goldfish!" shouted Natalie.

"Look over there sunshine. It looks like an airplane!" Fred said warmly.

"Dad, I could have a job using special airplanes to make beautiful clouds," beamed Natalie.

"Natalie, did you know there's a career in the field of science called meteorology?

A meteorologist advises people about the weather such as sunny days like today." said Fred.

"You could be a dentist and help ensure that everyone has healthy teeth." said Fred.

Natalie responded "I like our dentist, but he doesn't let me have candy.

If I was a dentist, I would give candy to every kid, like a candy superhero!"

Fred laughed and said "Natalie, too much candy is bad for your teeth.

That is why the dentist doesn't recommend that you have so much.

He wants you to have strong and healthy teeth."

"Dad, look at those beautiful roses. I wish I had flowers that would match my outfits.

Is there any career where I could do something like that?" wished Natalie.

Fred thought for a while and said "Computer programmers create apps that help people everywhere."

"Do you think there is an app for picking flowers that will always match my clothes?" Natalie asked.

"I am not sure sunshine, but I think you are getting the hang of this career thing," Fred proudly stated.

"Natalie, do you like Mrs. Hughes? You could be a teacher like her." Fred said.

"Everyone likes Mrs. Hughes. She is very smart and a wonderful teacher." Natalie responded.

After a few moments and some thoughtful thinking Natalie said,

"I would like to teach, train, and also race giraffes. I really like giraffes a lot!"

Fred laughed and scooped Natalie up for a race back to the car.

"Natalie, you can be whatever you want as long as you are passionate and work hard to be the best you can.

Once you decide to do something you love, you will be happy, and it will never get boring," stated Fred.

"Thanks, Dad. You're the best," said Natalie.

"So, what are you going to draw for your assignment?" Fred asked.

Natalie smiled and looked out the window thinking of all the possibilities.

It was Monday morning, and Mrs. Hughes looked forward to seeing the children's assignments.

"Good morning children, how was your weekend?" asked Mrs. Hughes.

"It was good, Mrs. Hughes." The classroom of first graders all chorused.

"How many of you were able to do the assignment I gave you?" Mrs. Hughes asked as several hands went up.

"Natalie, let's start with you. What would you like to be when you grow up?" inquired Mrs. Hughes.

Natalie walked to the front of the class and presented a picture she had painted herself.

Pointing at the picture, Natalie said: "My dad helped with my assignment and he told me,

I could be whatever I wanted to be as long as I work hard and I am passionate about my job."

"So, when I grow up I want to be a good parent like my dad and also have lots and lots of giraffes.

I want to work hard teaching the giraffes about all the possible careers for when they grow up!"

www.ingramcontent.com/pod-product-compliance
Lightning Source LLC
Chambersburg PA
CBHW041239040426

42445CB00004B/91